OUR PRESIDENT
DONALD TRUMP

CREATED BY WILDER FREEDOM

© 2024 Wilder Freedom
Published by Conscious Mothers
All rights reserved.

First Edition, 2024

No part of this publication may be reproduced, distributed, or transmitted in any form or by any means, including photocopying, recording, or other electronic or mechanical methods, without the prior written permission of the publisher, except in the case of brief quotations embodied in critical reviews and certain other noncommercial uses permitted by copyright law.

DISCLAIMER AND NOTICES

This is an independently authored children's book designed to help young readers understand historical events and encourage discussions about American leadership and democracy. While based on public records and historical events, this work represents the author's creative interpretation for educational purposes.

This book is a work of creative expression and is not endorsed by, approved by, or affiliated with Donald Trump, the Trump Organization, the U.S. government, or any governmental entity. Any references to historical events, public figures, or governmental institutions are included solely for educational and illustrative purposes.

ABOUT THE ILLUSTRATIONS

The illustrations in this book are original artistic interpretations created using artificial intelligence technology. These watercolor-style images are not photographs or official representations. All illustrations are created specifically for this educational children's book and are designed to complement the biographical narrative in an age-appropriate manner. The images, including any representations of official symbols, are used for artistic and illustrative purposes only.

EDUCATIONAL PURPOSE

This book is intended as an educational resource to help children understand contemporary American history and leadership. It is not intended to influence political views or represent any official positions. The content is presented in an age-appropriate manner to encourage family discussions about civic engagement, perseverance, and American democracy.

ISBN: 978-1-7638045-0-0

www.facebook.com/wilderfreedomauthor

*For the American People—
whose voices shape our nation's story
through the sacred right to vote.*

Once upon a time, in the bustling city of New York, a little boy named Donald was born. He lived among towering buildings that seemed to touch the clouds, and streets filled with people chasing their dreams.

Little Donald had a special dream of his own—he loved to build things! He would stack blocks higher and higher, imagining they were giant buildings touching the sky. "Someday," he would say, "I'm going to build the most beautiful buildings anyone has ever seen!"

As Donald grew up, he worked very hard to make his dream come true. He learned about construction, design, and business. Soon, he was building real buildings—tall, shiny skyscrapers that sparkled in the sunlight and fancy hotels where people could stay while visiting exciting places. His buildings became famous all around the world!

But Donald had an even bigger dream growing in his heart. He looked around at his country, America, and thought about how he could help make it better. "Maybe," he thought, "I could be President and help make America the best it could be!"

"I LIKE THINKING BIG. IF YOU'RE GOING TO BE THINKING ANYTHING, YOU MIGHT AS WELL THINK BIG."

- Donald Trump, 1987

Some people laughed because Donald wasn't a regular politician—he was a builder and a businessman! But Donald remembered what he learned as a little boy: dreams come true if you work hard and never give up. He was like a lion, brave and strong, roaring loudly for what he believed was right.

He traveled across America, talking to people about his ideas. He wanted to create more jobs, keep the country safe, and help people chase their own dreams. Many people liked what he said, and in 2016, something amazing happened - Donald Trump was elected the 45th President of the United States!

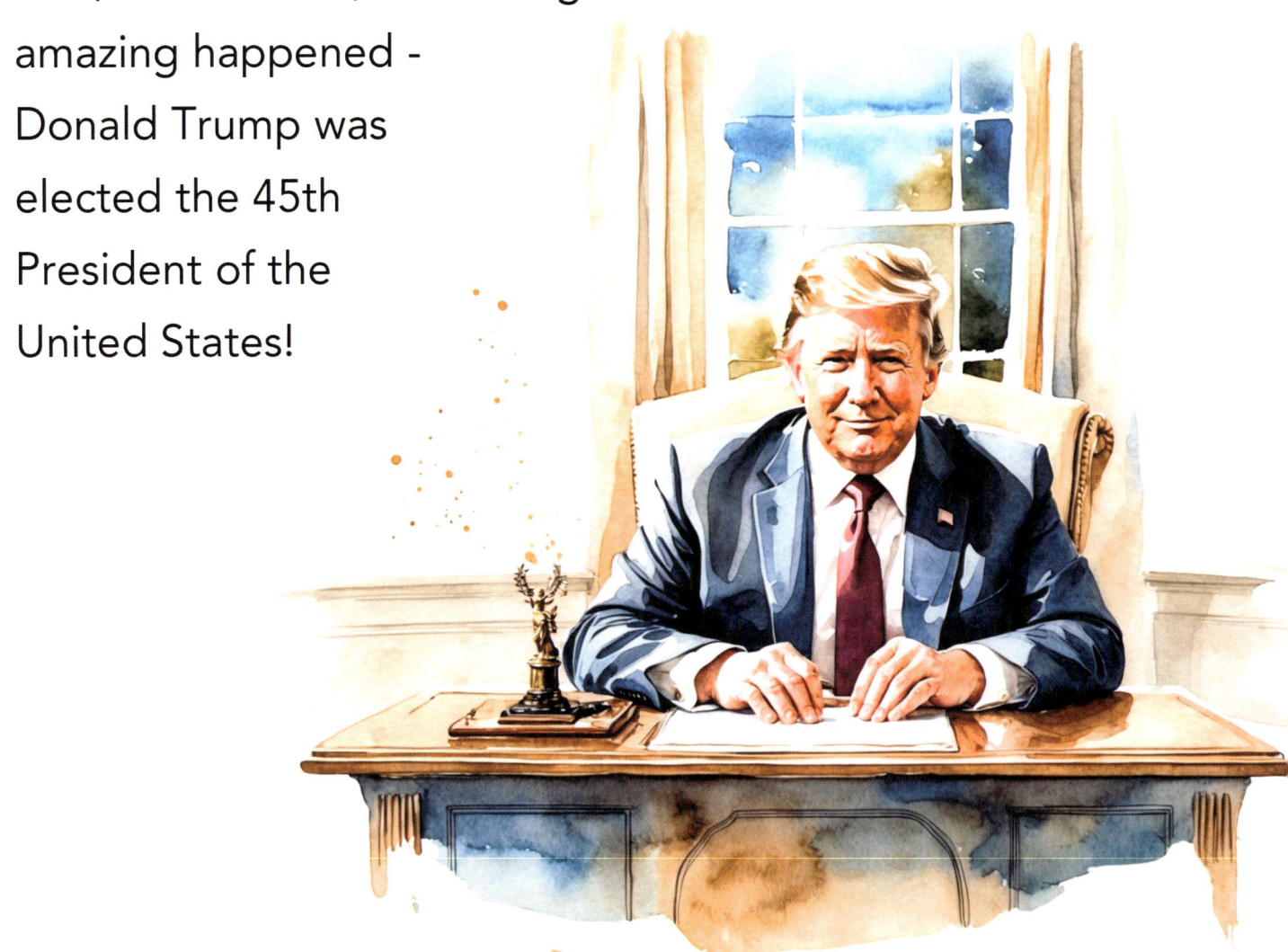

"THE FORGOTTEN MEN AND WOMEN OF OUR COUNTRY WILL BE FORGOTTEN NO LONGER."

- Donald Trump, 2016

"AMERICA WILL COME BACK BIGGER, BETTER, AND STRONGER THAN EVER BEFORE."

- Donald Trump, 2023

As President, Donald was different from those who came before him. He was like a builder with a toolbox full of new ideas. He wanted America to grow strong and proud, like a tree with deep roots that stays steady no matter what happens. His family—wife Melania and his five children—stood by his side, supporting him every step of the way.

"WE'RE GOING TO BRING BACK JOBS, BRING BACK WEALTH, AND BRING BACK OUR DREAM"

- Donald Trump, 2017

"I'M FIGHTING FOR YOU, AND I WILL CONTINUE TO FIGHT FOR YOU."

- Donald Trump, 2020

Some people really liked his bold way of talking and doing things, while others didn't agree with him. But that's okay—in America, we can all have different opinions! What mattered most was that Donald always told people to stand tall and believe in themselves.

Donald worked hard to keep his promises. He wanted to make sure American families had good jobs and felt safe in their homes. His special motto was "Make America Great Again," which reminded people of their own dreams and hopes for the future.

"WE WILL NEVER SURRENDER OUR LIBERTY, OUR FREEDOM, OR OUR WAY OF LIFE."

- Donald Trump, 2020

In 2024, something exciting happened! Just like that little boy who never gave up on his dream of building tall buildings, Donald was elected president again. He promised to keep working hard for all the families and children across America, helping them build their own dreams too.

The most important lesson from Donald's story is that you should always believe in yourself, even when others doubt you. Whether you want to construct skyscrapers, lead the nation, or chase any other dream—with persistence and dedication, extraordinary things are possible!

"THIS IS GOING TO BE THE GOLDEN AGE OF AMERICA, WHICH WILL ALLOW US TO MAKE AMERICA GREAT AGAIN!"

- Donald Trump, 2024

Donald J. Trump's journey teaches us that with courage, hard work, and a love for our country, we can all make a difference. No matter where you're from or what your aspirations are, remember that America is a land of hope, freedom, and opportunity for everyone!

Exploring Big Dreams Together

Family Discussion Guide
Questions for Young Explorers

What is YOUR biggest dream right now?
- Draw or describe something you want to accomplish

Can you think of a time when someone told you that you couldn't do something?
- How did you feel?
- Did you keep trying anyway?

What does "working hard" look like to you?
- Share a story about a time you or someone you know worked really hard to achieve a goal

Exploring Big Dreams Together

Family Discussion Guide
Questions for Young Explorers

> What does being a good leader mean to you?
> • Name three qualities of a good leader
> • Who is a leader you admire?

> What makes you proud to be an American?
> • What opportunities do you see around you?
> • How can you help your community?

Encourage curiosity, listen actively, and celebrate your child's unique dreams and path!

www.ingramcontent.com/pod-product-compliance
Lightning Source LLC
Chambersburg PA
CBRC091724070526
44585CB00008B/168